ANIMALS AT RISK

# TASMANIAN DEVILS IN DANGER

BY MICHAEL PORTMAN

**Please visit our website, www.garethstevens.com. For a free color catalog of all our high-quality books, call toll free 1-800-542-2595 or fax 1-877-542-2596.**

**Library of Congress Cataloging-in-Publication Data**

Portman, Michael, 1976-
Tasmanian devils in danger / Michael Portman.
p. cm. — (Animals at risk)
Includes index.
ISBN 978-1-4339-5808-3 (pbk.)
ISBN 978-1-4339-5809-0 (6-pack)
ISBN 978-1-4339-5806-9 (library binding)
1. Tasmanian devil—Juvenile literature. 2. Endangered species—Juvenile literature. I. Title.
QL737.M33P67 2012
599.2'7—dc22

2011006075

First Edition

Published in 2012 by
**Gareth Stevens Publishing**
111 East 14th Street, Suite 349
New York, NY 10003



Designer: Haley W. Harasymiw
Editor: Therese M. Shea

Photo credits: Cover, pp. 1, 5, 9, 10, 11, 15, 19 Shutterstock.com; p. 7 Brendon Thorne/Getty Images; p. 13 Jason Edwards/National Geographic/Getty Images; p. 17 Adam Petty/Getty Images.



Printed in the United States of America

CPSIA compliance information: Batch #CS11GS: For further information contact Gareth Stevens, New York, New York at 1-800-542-2595.

# Contents



Words in the glossary appear in **bold** type the first time they are used in the text.

# Meet the Tasmanian Devil

The Tasmanian devil is one of the rarest and most unusual animals in the world. When many people think of a Tasmanian devil, they think of the growling, cranky cartoon animal. The real Tasmanian devil isn't much different!

Tasmanian devils live on the island of Tasmania, just south of Australia. This is the only place in the world where Tasmanian devils can be found in the wild. They are tough and **feisty** animals. However, today they're struggling just to **survive**.

WILD FACTS

Before Tasmanian devils fight, they often make a sneezing noise to scare away their enemies.

Over 400 years ago, Tasmanian devils lived on the mainland of Australia.

# Little Devils

Tasmanian devils are marsupials, which means the females have a pouch for carrying their babies. A baby Tasmanian devil is called a joey. When joeys are born, they're about the size of a raisin. A female Tasmanian devil can give birth to as many as 50 joeys at one time, but only four or fewer will survive.

At first, joeys are hairless. They later grow short brown or black fur. An adult Tasmanian devil usually has white patches on its chest and rear end, too.

Joeys come out of their mother's pouch after about 4 months.

# Night Hunters

Tasmanian devils are nocturnal, which means they sleep during the day and look for food at night. They eat only meat. The Tasmanian devil is the largest meat-eating marsupial in the world.

With sharp teeth and strong **jaws**, Tasmanian devils have one of the most powerful bites of any animal. They're excellent hunters. When a Tasmanian devil finds a meal, it eats every part of it—even fur and bones! However, it's mainly a **scavenger** and eats whatever meat it comes across, dead or alive.

Tasmanian devils prefer to live in forests but will travel to find food.

# Cranky Critter

The Tasmanian devil got its name because of the screeching and growling noises it makes. These fierce fighters snap and bite when they think they're in danger. Most of the time, they prefer not to fight. They'd rather scare their enemies away. Tasmanian devils also give off a strong smell when they're scared or angry.

Tasmanian devils spend most of their lives alone. They come together to **mate** and sometimes to feed. The forest can get noisy when several Tasmanian devils are fighting over a meal!

Sometimes when facing an enemy, a Tasmanian devil yawns—almost as if it's bored!

## WILD FACTS

Tasmanian devils store fat in their tails. A well-fed Tasmanian devil has a thick tail.

# A Price on Their Heads

When the first European settlers moved to Tasmania, they treated Tasmanian devils like pests. Tasmanian devils can kill animals larger than themselves, such as sheep. However, they mostly kill smaller animals or animals caught in traps. Still, farmers saw them as a **threat** to their livestock.

In the 1800s, people began offering bounties, or rewards, for Tasmanian devils. So many of them were killed that they were in danger of becoming **extinct**. In 1941, a law was passed to protect Tasmanian devils.

**WILD FACTS**

Farmers today value Tasmanian devils because they eat mice that eat crops.

When Tasmanian devils aren't hunting, they find shelter in logs, caves, and other dens.

# More Threats

Even as a protected **species**, Tasmanian devils face dangers. Since they're scavengers, they eat animals that have been struck by cars and trucks. As a result, many Tasmanian devils are killed on roads. They also **compete** with each other and with other animals for food. There often isn't enough food to keep them all healthy.

Even so, the Tasmanian devil population began to increase after 1941. By the mid-1990s, scientists thought there were as many as 250,000 Tasmanian devils. However, the biggest threat of all was yet to come.

When a Tasmanian devil gets excited, its ears turn red.

# Deadly Disease

In 1996, scientists began to notice something strange happening to some Tasmanian devils. Their faces were covered in large growths called tumors. Scientists discovered that the animals were suffering from a **disease**. They named it devil **facial** tumor disease, or DFTD.

Once a Tasmanian devil has DFTD, its mouth becomes filled with tumors. This makes it impossible for the animal to eat. A Tasmanian devil with DFTD dies within a few months. DFTD spreads when an animal with the disease bites another animal.

Scientists gather facts about Tasmanian devils in the wild so they can work toward new ways to keep them healthy.

# Glimmer of Hope

Devil facial tumor disease is spreading fast. There are now as few as 2,000 Tasmanian devils left in the wild. Sadly, there's no cure for DFTD. Wild Tasmanian devils face the possibility of extinction. However, there is hope.

Over the past several years, special areas called sanctuaries have been set aside for Tasmanian devils that don't suffer from DFTD. These healthy Tasmanian devils have a chance to increase their population. If wild Tasmanian devils do become extinct, scientists hope the animals in sanctuaries will help the species survive.

**WILD FACTS**

Since 1996, 90 percent of wild Tasmanian devils have died of DFTD.

There may be as many as nine kinds of DFTD, which makes the search for a cure even harder.

# The Future

The Tasmanian devil once faced the threat of extinction because of people's actions. Today, it's a prized **symbol** of the Tasmania National Parks and Wildlife Service.

A cure for the deadly devil facial tumor disease is still many years away. The governments of Australia and Tasmania provide money to scientists to beat DFTD. In addition, a sanctuary in Australia called Devil Ark was built to house 1,000 healthy Tasmanian devils. Hopeful animal lovers will fight for the survival of the Tasmanian devil.

## Facts About Tasmanian Devils

| | |
|---|---|
| Length | 23–26 inches (58–66 cm) |
| Weight | 13–18 pounds (6–8 kg) |
| Life Span | 7–8 years in the wild |

# Glossary

**compete:** to try to do something better

**disease:** an illness

**extinct:** having no living members

**facial:** having to do with the face

**feisty:** ready to attack or fight

**jaw:** one of the two bones in which teeth are set

**mate:** to come together to produce babies

**scavenger:** an animal that eats the remains of dead animals

**species:** a group of animals that are all of the same kind

**survive:** to stay alive

**symbol:** something that stands for something else

**threat:** something likely to cause harm

# For More Information

## Books

Hengel, Katherine. *It's a Baby Tasmanian Devil!* Edina, MN: ABDO Publishing, 2010.

Sirota, Lyn A. *Tasmanian Devils.* Mankato, MN: Capstone Press, 2010.

## Websites

**Devil Ark**
*www.devilark.com.au*
Learn about what's being done to help save Tasmanian devils.

**Mammals: Tasmanian Devil**
*www.sandiegozoo.org/animalbytes/t-tasmanian_devil.html*
Read fun facts about Tasmanian devils.

**Tasmanian Devils**
*kids.nationalgeographic.com/kids/animals/creaturefeature/tasmanian-devil*
Watch a video about Tasmanian devils.

# INDEX